HAUT GOÛT

Allan Havis

BROADWAY PLAY PUBLISHING INC
224 E 62nd St, NY, NY 10065
www.broadwayplaypub.com
info@broadwayplaypub.com

HAUT GOÛT

© Copyright 2013 by Allan Havis

All rights reserved. This work is fully protected under the copyright laws of the United States of America. No part of this publication may be photocopied, reproduced, stored in a retrieval system, or transmitted, in any form or by any means, electronic, mechanical, recording, or otherwise, without the prior permission of the publisher. Additional copies of this play are available from the publisher.

Written permission is required for live performance of any sort. This includes readings, cuttings, scenes, and excerpts. For amateur and stock performances, please contact Broadway Play Publishing Inc. For all other rights contact Susan Schulman, A Literary Agency, 454 W 44th St, NY NY 10036, 212 713-1633, fax 212 581-8830, Schulman@aol.com.

First printing: April 2013
I S B N: 978-0-88145-551-9

Book design: Marie Donovan
Page make-up: Adobe Indesign
Typeface: Palatino
Printed and bound in the U S A

HAUT GOÛT was first produced by Virginia Stage Company in April 1987. The cast and creative contributors were:

DR JULES GOLD	Danton Stone
DR LUDWIG FURST	Humbert Allen Astredo
JO ANNE GOLD	Gordana Rashovich
SHIRLEY FURST	Helen Harrelson
LE CROIX	Lou Meyers
MATI	Valerie Brandon
LATCH	Tom Rolfing
Director	Christopher Hanna

An earlier version of HAUT GOÛT was developed at the Sundance Institute Playwrights Laboratory in the summer of 1986. Subsequent to the Virginia Stage production, the play had its West Coast premiere at South Coast Repertory in September and October 1987. The cast and creative contributors were:

DR JULES GOLD	Charles Lanyer
DR LUDWIG FURST	John-David Keller
JO ANNE GOLD	Anni Long
SHIRLEY FURST	Sally Kemp
LE CROIX	Ben Halley Jr
MATI	Adrienne Morgan
LATCH	Michael Canavan
Director	Jody McAuliffe

CHARACTERS & SETTING

DR JULES GOLD, *suburban internist at a Westchester hospital, middle age but youthful. Serious manner, crisp speech, a political liberal, preoccupied with his zeal for work and recognition.*

DR LUDWIG FURST, GOLD's *senior hospital colleague, age mid 60s. German accent, devious sense of humor, a faux-bigot with a warm interior.*

JO ANNE, GOLD's *wife, late 30s. Attractive, patient, caring and balanced mother of two pre-teens.*

SHIRLEY, FURST's *wife, late 50s or early 60s. Overweight and loosely dressed with fabrics. She sees herself as a clairvoyant and an important force in GOLD's life and marriage.*

LE CROIX, *Haitian Army General, mid 50s, formidable air, and on the surface mercurial in his swings from playful to terrifying. Heroin addict and enduring a grave medical illness.*

MATI, *a Haitian Mombo—practitioner of magic. She is a thin, forbidding woman with strong presence.*

LATCH, *State Department official. Casual manner, presumptuous, and dresses in Bill Blass leisure wear.*

Time: Present

Place: Scarsdale, New York and in and around Port-au-Prince, Haiti

The publication of HAUT GOÛT in 2012 was an opportunity to revisit the play's text, introduce some cuts, and flag the various cultural and political references from the 1980s. Certainly, Haiti's economic suffering hasn't changed in the span of twenty-five years, although there have been pockets of political reform since the days of the Duvalier family's stranglehold on the tiny nation. During the 1980s, Haiti postured against communism to please the United States and the Reagan Administration, but Jean-Claude "Baby Doc" Duvalier's excesses, playboy life, and arrogance only diminished Haiti's health. His father, François "Papa Doc" Duvalier had ruled with an iron hand, using a purged military and voodoo mystique which led to the murder of roughly 30,000 Haitians and an exodus of Haiti's professional class to other nations. Surprising the world, Jean-Claude Duvalier returned to Port-au-Prince in January 2011 after two decades of self-imposed exile in France. He was immediately arrested by Haitian police and charged with embezzlement. In the *2004 Global Transparency Report*, Duvalier was vaulted into the list of the World's All-Time Most Corrupt Leaders in the World. François Duvalier's son was listed sixth and having amassed between $300 million to $800 million dollars. The devastating 7.0 earthquake which hit Haiti in January 2010 impacted over three million people. The Haitian government reported that an estimated 316,000 people had died, 300,000 had been injured, and 1,000,000 made homeless. Without changing the story, this updated version of HAUT GOÛT is therefore set in the aftermath of the earthquake and Duvalier's jailing.

Scene One

(DR GOLD's *Scarsdale, New York home. A view of the garden can be seen off the living room. Modern art on the walls. The space connotes rich, austere taste.* FURST *and* GOLD *are at the bar.*)

GOLD: Is that your idea of mercy?

FURST: Hardly.

GOLD: What did they teach you in theology class?

FURST: Jules, you know I didn't attend those classes. Theology is for people who wear long morbid robes, like darling Shirley.

GOLD: *(Pouring* FURST *a drink)* Theology enriched me...

FURST: Brought out your brilliance.

GOLD: Yes, so to escape Bronxville and my mother's cooking, I earned a Rhodes Scholarship to Oxford. And my mother came along, Ludwig.

FURST: Yes, the über-Jewish mother. Like you, I was a gifted student, but I only cared to make money as swiftly as possible. Now I've a fat belly and three warring malpractice lawyers trying to guess my net worth.

GOLD: The world has changed.

FURST: Indeed, no respect for doctors. We used to walk the earth like gods.

GOLD: Now we have chauffeurs.

FURST: Do you watch morning television, Jules?

GOLD: No.

FURST: They ridicule us, Julies. Medical negligence, sex scandals, pension fraud, medicare scams, botox kickbacks, Obamacare...will it ever end? And I miss Oprah.

GOLD: Retire, Ludwig. I'll fill your shoes.

FURST: You lack cynicism.

GOLD: I can fake it.

FURST: Some things you can't fake. Medicine cannot be socialized. Health care is a privilege in today's overpopulated world. Spend a year in a government hospital, Jules.

GOLD: I have. We're ready for single payer health insurance.

FURST: It's an insidious form of communism, like food stamps and Tupperware parties.

GOLD: You're sounding like a crank.

FURST: I am a crank.

GOLD: I need a favor, Ludwig.

FURST: Not now. Ply me with your best liquor.

GOLD: You know what I'm about to ask.

FURST: Yes, your secretary told me. (*Abrupt switch*) Every society is divided into classes. One chooses with care the class which makes one happiest. It is a choice. We're not born into fate. You've chosen your class, Jules, as you've chosen your Porsches, your Armani suits, and winter vacations. We're of the privileged class, thank God.

GOLD: And God is pleased?

FURST: God is very pleased. Where are they now?

GOLD: Touring the garden. Jo Anne has landscaped again.

FURST: What talent she has.

GOLD: She's strip mined the azalea beds and our neighbors think we're fracking for natural gas. Twenty-seven thousand dollars later, I can't decide whether she designed miniature golf or a sanctuary for Trappist monks.

FURST: Better she stay in the garden than out of your sight. You run your home very well. Shirley's uncontrollable.

GOLD: Buy her a spade and a compost pile.

FURST: She doesn't have the patience for physical things.

GOLD: Shirley's spirited, yes.

FURST: Her sixth sense? Your diplomacy, I admire. I like your cleverness, Jules. I covet your beautiful wife, your darling children, your rising star has no limits. *(Holds up glass)* Another shot.

(GOLD pours)

FURST: I toast my young protégé. Doctor Gold. So eponymous. My protean wunderkind.

GOLD: Doctor Feelgood.

FURST: Doctor Spentwell. Doctor Jules Morris Gold, who loves patients like family, and treats family like patients.

GOLD: Please.

FURST: I could rant about your diabolic golf game or your once celebrated cocaine habit.

GOLD: You were addicted to Percocet.

FURST: Only if you chase it with single malt scotch, Jules. My generation prefers scotch in our battles with depression.

GOLD: I never suffered depression.

FURST: Nor I, though my face appears melancholic. Sardonic mudslide smiles, fighting the marital pains that erode the jowls of my clay-baked mask. It is said, you know, that every deceased doctor mars the human face. We aren't supposed to die. Aren't you drinking with me?

GOLD: On call tonight at the hospital.

FURST: Tonight of all nights?

GOLD: A favor to Schyler.

FURST: So responsible of you. You are the perfect image of the austere Jewish saint, never a pound overweight nor a hair out of place. Mercy, mercy, mercy, if we could grant absolution to our patients, Jules, if we could provide the ointment to the dull cancer inside the soul, if we could act like priest, rabbi and sage all in one, we could charge a little more.

GOLD: You're a carpet bagger.

FURST: Not true.

GOLD: A foreigner, Ludwig.

FURST: (*Masking his German accent with a Texas twang*) I am thoroughly red-blooded American, I can assure you. Do you really want hacks from Pakistan and Costa Rica in our ward? They're taking over our hospital beds, our parking spaces, our cabanas at the country club. Do I sound like a bigot? One must have a correct sense of prejudices. I've no love for quotas.

(*Sensing* GOLD's *discomfort*)

FURST: Do I mistreat you at staff meetings, Jules? It's how I show favoritism.

GOLD: Spare me then.

FURST: When you support Third World medical schools and untested exchange doctors, yes...I have to slap some sense into you in front of others. Oh, hell, pick up your drink. This was supposed to be a special occasion. Your fortieth birthday? Your fiftieth? Your age is an enigma.

GOLD: Ludwig, about this request.

FURST: Name it, for Christsakes.

GOLD: Give me a leave of absence. For my research grant. At the most, four months. This is the...

FURST:...most important project of your career.

GOLD: The Health Institute's providing everything I need, no strings attached.

FURST: Four months, too long.

GOLD: Honor this project, Ludwig.

FURST: You're my right hand at the hospital.

GOLD: Schyler can fill in for me.

FURST: No, he can't. He's a putz!

GOLD: My milk formula must be tested.

FURST: Hire some flunky to test it.

GOLD: There are too many variables to worry over. The first step against infant mortality in the underdeveloped world.

FURST: You know, Jules, I've always stressed breast-feeding. Especially for delinquents. It's the tactile thing. I was breast-fed by a beautiful neighbor in Stuttgart. It was the finest relation of my life. Have you reinvented the breast, Jules?

GOLD: I have.

FURST: I'm not letting you go.

GOLD: You're not going to stand in my way. I'm years ahead of other researchers from Nestlé. Why begrudge me?

FURST: My generous German instinct. Zugzwang. You cannot move.

GOLD: You're jealous.

FURST: Perhaps I am.

GOLD: I'll share credit when the publicity breaks.

FURST: Don't make my life any harder.

(JO ANNE *enters with hors d'oeuvres.*)

JO ANNE: Did you forget us outside?

FURST: Never.

GOLD: Are the children in bed?

JO ANNE: Yes. Come and join us.

GOLD: Give us just a minute.

JO ANNE: Should I guess the subject?

GOLD: Ludwig's blood pressure is up.

FURST: Take my pulse, Jo Anne.

(JO ANNE *obliges* FURST.)

FURST: What warm hands, my dear.

JO ANNE: Don't make me lose count.

FURST: Count backwards, like the astronauts.

JO ANNE: A rapid pulse.

FURST: It's your radiant presence. Is the moon out tonight?

JO ANNE: Come and look.

FURST: I should have been a gynecologist, Jules.

GOLD: Your hands are too cold.

FURST: Or perhaps a musician with dreadlocks in a reggae band from Trenchtown? Where is my wife?

JO ANNE: In the garden.

FURST: Never leave her alone. She hears voices. Michael Jackson. Whitney Houston. Dead pop singers.

JO ANNE: Shirley loves music.

FURST: Yes, I tend to persecute her during her brief periods of lucidity while she hears music. It's as if the occult invented this woman.

JO ANNE: Misogyny is so dated, Ludwig.

FURST: What cheap liquor. Jules refuses to show me the label.

GOLD: J & B. Jewish booze.

JO ANNE: Jules must use the grant immediately.

GOLD: She's right, Ludwig.

FURST: Gold's milk. God's milk?

GOLD: The formula is beyond criticism, Ludwig.

FURST: How modest, Jules.

GOLD: I can afford a little immodesty.

FURST: Spare us. Bright lights knock me out.

GOLD: If you won't relent, I'll quit the hospital.

FURST: Jules, I'm thinking about your family. You're not a bachelor.

GOLD: Jo Anne's behind me.

FURST: Is she?

JO ANNE: Jules...

FURST: My decision rests with your dear wife. If she is willing to indulge you...

JO ANNE: Jules...

GOLD: Don't say anything now.

JO ANNE: *(Approaching him)*Hold me, Jules. Pretend we're alone. Then say what you want.

GOLD: You want to please Ludwig.

JO ANNE: Only by having him see us as were years ago. Like the photo-shop family album on your desk.

GOLD: *(Obliging her)* Like this?

JO ANNE: See, Ludwig's smiling.

FURST: I am.

GOLD: An authentic smile?

FURST: As authentic as my accent. Tell me truthfully, do you love your wife?

GOLD: Without this angel, I might as well be in Dante's Inferno.

JO ANNE: He once said this on our honeymoon.

GOLD: Because you were an angel.

JO ANNE: Though angels never cry.

GOLD: They simply dance on the head of a pin.

JO ANNE: *(Playing with his hair)* We ought to go dancing tonight.

GOLD: You know I can't dance.

JO ANNE: Jules, a dancer you were meant to be. In top hat and tails, gliding down a thousand magic stairs, sweeping me off to ports unknown. Be my romantic fantasy tonight. Be mine.

(JO ANNE *kisses* GOLD *delicately and he responds. They embrace for a slow-motion dance.)*

FURST: Dear Lord, I must be aroused. Where is my dancing partner?

(FURST *exits.* JO ANNE *and* GOLD *remain in embrace)*

JO ANNE : We should dance more often.

GOLD: Dancing is for strangers.

JO ANNE: Are we strangers?

GOLD: Darling, you look stunning tonight. *(Kisses her slowly)*

JO ANNE: Make me happy.

GOLD: How can I make you happy?

JO ANNE: Postpone the trip. Or share this project with someone who has no family.

GOLD: There's no one I trust to make this work.

JO ANNE: I could jump in bed with you right now. Don't you get it, Jules?

GOLD: I do. The children are provided for. I'll be back before they even miss me. You said you would fly to Haiti before long.

JO ANNE: Visiting for a weekend is not the compromise.

GOLD: I'll fly back a few times too. You're wedded to Scarsdale.

JO ANNE: You want to get away. A change...

GOLD: A change would do us a world of good. An opportunity of this magnitude comes once in a career.

JO ANNE: Knowing you, time will drift. Your quiet obsessions will grow, the forgetful lapses, your F T D roses two weeks after my birthday.

GOLD: Then make the trip with me. We'll have your mother stay with the kids. I think that could work just as well.

JO ANNE: Is that an invitation, Jules?

GOLD: It is.

JO ANNE: My mother can't parachute in just like that. None of us have the freedom you have.

GOLD: This is the last favor I'll ever ask you.

JO ANNE: Maybe it is. You look at me differently, Jules. Are you aware of it? As though you were in surgery. So dispassionately. When I enter a room. I don't like it. You're acting like a dreamer.

GOLD: Perhaps I am a dreamer. Some men are built that way.

JO ANNE: Some men grow up. Some men stay home.

(FURST *enters.*)

GOLD: Please darling. If I don't get this patent, I'll rue this forever.

(*They stare at each other.*)

FURST: I found Shirley on the terrace lip-synching to Fellini's Juliet of the Spirits. I do hope the neighbors don't complain.

(JO ANNE, *kissing* FURST *on the cheek, exits past him.*)

FURST: We live for women, Jules, isn't that so? And you have my unabashed envy. I won't stand in your way.

GOLD: Thank you for this favor. You're quite generous.

FURST: Yes, I am. I certainly am. Trading compliments is easier than trading spouses. Spouse is such an ugly word. The etymology crosses sponge and louse in perfect balance. No gender to the word because torture knows no gender. God created marriage to restore our faith in divine retribution. At least you're happily married, my boy.

GOLD: Yes.

FURST: With more emotion, Jules.

GOLD: Yes.

FURST: Though you act like alone. You belong in the Yukon with a dog sled, jug of brandy, and the complete works of Graham Greene. You twisted her arm. I know.

GOLD: She talks to you?

FURST: Yes.

GOLD: And what does she tell you?

FURST: Your sexual appetite is waning.

GOLD: Do you pump her for information?

FURST: No. We men tire of our wives. Fact of nature. Marriages run in cycles, like washing machines. Perhaps the European tradition would suit you. You find a mistress far away from home. Or those high-class hookers from the Backpage website. Or telephone sex. Jules, do you understand that practice?

GOLD: You unscrew the receiver.

FURST: Do you expect great profits from your milk study?

GOLD: Yes, and I'm donating the proceeds to the International Red Cross.

FURST: You are the paragon of Social Responsibility. Heir to Roosevelt in the age of Wall Street bailouts. You pick my brains for political information, win a grant, and desert me. Take Jo Anne along, Jules. It's the wise thing to do. And don't stay a day longer than necessary. Jewish physicians shouldn't parade as Christian missionaries. The world is our Diaspora. Where in the Caribbean are you going?

GOLD: Haiti.

FURST: The poorest country in our hemisphere.

GOLD: They haven't recovered from the 2010 earthquake. Three hundred thousand still homeless. It's beyond shocking.

FURST: And yet the F D A wants the test conducted there?

GOLD: Why the hell not?

FURST: I wish you well, Jules. Save the children, it's in your heart. I'm giving you two months only. Because you're like a son to me. I wanted a son. *(He touches* GOLD *and this is the best he can manage to show tenderness)* Don't eat the local shellfish.

*(*SHIRLEY *and* JO ANNE *enter)*

FURST: Is that my wife? Come, Shirley, sit by me. Jules just told me the latest in dietetic aphrodisiacs. Shall we try some?

SHIRLEY: Whatever darling. Only bowel movements seem to rouse you lately.

FURST: How nice if you could rouse me.

SHIRLEY: It would take the magic of Lazarus and six blue pills. *(Kiss him, smiles to others)* The only physician on the East Coast who goes into the operating room with a rabbit's foot.

FURST: Jo Anne, defend me!

JO ANNE: Retreat. Dinner's ready.

FURST: Has Shirley heard voices tonight?

SHIRLEY: Has Ludwig been drinking tonight?

FURST: Spirits, demons, disembodied souls...none have phoned you today, Shirley? Show us your cell phone?

SHIRLEY: No voices, no texts.

FURST: Well, that is good news. We won't be tormented by the dead.

SHIRLEY: Those voices, darling, are your former patients.

FURST: How delightful. Tell them to return to their graves. With Shirley, every day is Halloween.

SHIRLEY: With Ludwig, every day is Yom Kippur.

FURST: Down, beast, down. *(Kisses her)* Did you know that Jules will be going to Haiti on a major grant?

SHIRLEY: Yes. When, Jules?

GOLD: A week from tomorrow.

SHIRLEY: You should have consulted me first.

GOLD: I'm sorry, Shirley.

JO ANNE: He's doing everything on his own.

SHIRLEY: How thoughtless, Jules. You used to seek my counsel. Our husbands are self-centered, aren't they? They walk around with blinking, beeping pagers, and their emergency I D cards, and M D car plates, our little deities from Olympus.

GOLD: Actually I have you to thank. Of all people, you encouraged me to develop the infant formula.

SHIRLEY: You're always proving yourself and can't find a practical place in the middle. Research was something you needed to do. I was happy to cheer you on. But you can hand this off to a colleague. You must want to blaze like a shooting star. When were you in Washington?

GOLD: Last week.

SHIRLEY: You men with two men from the N I H and one of the men was in a wheelchair.

GOLD: Shirley, don't play Ouija board with me tonight. Yes, one scientist was in a wheelchair.

FURST: Humor her, my boy. Even if she's spot on.

SHIRLEY: I don't like these men, Jules.

GOLD: Why don't you like these men?

SHIRLEY: Their choice of clothes. They're very keen on you. Breakfast is a lovely time to make decisions. Make your decision tomorrow, Jules. For your wife's sake. Tonight we should just celebrate your birthday. Think of pleasant things. Brisses, Barbeques, Bar Mitzvahs.

GOLD: Very funny, Shirley.

SHIRLEY: Don't do anything rash. We want you around for a long time.

GOLD: For every decision you have a hunch.

SHIRLEY: I live for hunches, Jules.

GOLD: I live for science, Shirley.

SHIRLEY: You take your hubris from Ludwig, but you're not invulnerable. You're not like my Jewish Bismarck. Ludwig has tremendous armor. Your talents are softer and truer. Stay home. I wanted you to finish your project, to excel to your fullest, to lend your special gifts to the world. But pass the baton now. Let another doctor go for you. This is not the time. You know what I mean. Can't you feel it, Jules?

GOLD: I want this opportunity, Shirley. I can't wait for pretty pictures from your tarot deck.

FURST: Altruism in a strange land exacts a cost.

GOLD: I've weighed the costs. Really, you're all ganging up on me. This is a lifelong wish. A little fling with research. A birthday present in the Caribbean seas. A hospital ward with my name and authority.

JO ANNE: Go to Haiti, darling. Feed the world. God in Heave has you by the neck.

SHIRLEY: This isn't the season for benevolence. Milk is not champagne. Pain is not adventure. Your lofty ideals drug you. You risk more than the comforts of home. I feel a certain way and it frightens me so.

GOLD: I'm going to do what I damn well please.

SHIRLEY: Medicine won't absolve you, Jules, for things are never so easy. Your vanity is getting the better of you. I wish there were a cure for your faith in medicine.

FURST: Perfect benediction for leaving. Jules, make us proud of you. Get your name in the news. Become celebrated and famous. Become a god, our Good Humor man dressed in white with a cheery little hat and bell. A gift to the world. Our selfless Jewish savior from Westchester. *(Glass in air, toasting)* To the starving indigent Haitians and military fascists...to American air bases in the Caribbean...to Doctor Gold's magnificent milk.

Scene Two

(LE CROIX's office in Haiti. Six weeks later. December. Midday. GOLD stands at the doorway in a blindfold. LE CROIX looks out the window with binoculars. As in all the scenes in LE CROIX's office, MATI is present and silent. After a moment, she removes GOLD's blindfold.)

LE CROIX: Why are you late?

GOLD: My driver took the coastal route. Very scenic.

LE CROIX: Don't be shy, cousin. Come closer.

GOLD: I don't like blindfolds and being roughed up.

LE CROIX: My apologies. I must take precautions.

GOLD: I've other appointments today. I came as a favor.

LE CROIX: And I appreciate the favor. The children's hospital enjoys the army's protection. You did ask for protection?

GOLD: I did. There were many break-ins and thefts.

LE CROIX: Are your papers in order, Doctor?

GOLD: Everything's with your sentry.

LE CROIX: How young you look. From your dossier, I was expecting an older man.

GOLD: If this this an inconvenient time, I could come back.

LE CROIX: Sit down, Doctor Gold.

(GOLD *doesn't*.)

LE CROIX: Sit down. Have you had lunch?

GOLD: No.

LE CROIX: I can order in.

GOLD: No, thank you . General, I must make a request of you. We need more soldiers during the midnight shift. Two thieves broke in again. I can't continue with my work while we sit open to vandalism and looting.

LE CROIX: How old are you, Doctor?

GOLD: Does my age matter?

LE CROIX: Everything matters, man.

GOLD: I want ten good soldiers. Promise me.

LE CROIX: Of course, Doctor. You come highly recommended. I put in many requests for a physician of great ability. We combed the neighboring islands and our own. Your name was on top of the list. Congratulations. *(Pause)* I cannot afford publicity. We must be discreet.

GOLD: I don't have much time, General.

LE CROIX: I will watch the clock, not you. Don't ever forget that. I've much to do before the end ofth e year. It is a crucial year.

GOLD: You needn't confide to me. I don't want to get involved in your politics.i

LE CROIX: You're here, aren't you? *(Pause)* Doctor, if I had my way, I' rather disappear until fully cured. But my responsibilities are to the army, to the people's safety, and to the legend of the Tonton Macoutes. I must stay visible, in perfect virile health.

GOLD: You want me to treat you and I want certain services at the hospital. That is all I want. Realize I'm needed every minute at the hospital. You may be running half of the island, but my work comes first. Is that understood?

LE CROIX: You've a lot to learn, Doctor Gold. A lot to learn. Well, how do I look?

GOLD: All right.

LE CROIX: Speak freely, man. From this moment on you're my personal physician.

GOLD: You look anemic and sickly.

LE CROIX: Do I appear queer, feeble, a bit insane?

GOLD: I cannot say.

LE CROIX: Starved for love? *(Pause)* Humor me if you can, Doctor Gold. *(Perhaps lighting a cigar)* And I will humor you. Do you still like women? Are you happily married? Have you ever had a sexual disease? What causes poison ivy if you never hike? Hemorrhoids? Morning nausea? Look, look, at my lizard skin. *(Rolls up sleeve)* Little ugly blisters, scales inflamed. Have you a jell for me? Something relieve the shitty itching. Where is your black bag?

GOLD: Your sentry grabbed it from me.

LE CROIX: You will examine me today.

GOLD: *(Annoyed)* I'd like my bag.

LE CROIX: You have a gentle hand? Bring me good health and I'll make you a very happy man. Whatever your pleasure. Beyond money. Legal or something more exotic? I understand you like golf. Are you bothered that I'm a communist?

GOLD: It's rather irrelevant.

LE CROIX: No, I must disagree. No one loves a communist. Particularly, a black intellectual one who's agile with a riding crop. There's talk in all the bars and cares and the newspapers.

GOLD: I don't read the newspapers.

LE CROIX: I align myself with estranged nations and forces. You've heard, no doubt, that I run a special detention center for politicals?

GOLD: Yes, I know.

LE CROIX: The popular perception in Haiti has it that I'm excessively cruel and sadistic. But in truth, I'm just a fat, cuddly teddy bear. So palpable. Two ugly dimples when I smile. My auntie taught me how to smile, though it's an unnecessary feminine trait. *(Smiles and picks up phone)* Let me order food for us. *(On phone) Deux omelettes du fromage avec café! (Pause)* Six magic eggs for breakfast. Each egg a small prophecy. Save the shell. We give them to Mati. *(He indicates her)* What month were you born, Doctor?

GOLD: October. General, I really must get back to the hospital.

LE CROIX: Astrologically, we're compatible. Ask me why. Every year I receive a letter from your government asking for my exact date of birth. Will they send me a cake? *(Laughter)* Your government is ridiculous. They thought I slept with Fidel. Do you think that?

GOLD: We ought to begin with some family history.

LE CROIX: I HAVE NO FAMILY.

GOLD: No brothers and sisters?

LE CROIX: They were murdered a long time ago.

GOLD: Any prevalent illness from either parent?

LE CROIX: My mother was a chambermaid for a white clothing merchant. That was her only sickness. My father rolled cigars for a crooked Jew who sold cars. Let's dispense with these questions. My symptoms are not my parents' and my illness has no heritage.

GOLD: When was your last medical?

LE CROIX: I'm checked weekly by the army surgeons. Cold clammy hands, dirty toungue applicator, shitty disposition, gigantic proctoscope. Hernadez gave out vitamin-B pills and brutal enemas. I couldn't tolerate him. Ordered his execution.

GOLD: I may not suit you any better. Please get my bag.

(MATI *exits and returns with tray of food. Sets it down on desk.*)

LE CROIX: His black bag, Mati. Thank you.

(MATI *exits, having gazed at* GOLD. LE CROIX *smiles warmly.*)

LE CROIX: Do I strip to my feet?

GOLD: In a minute.

LE CROIX: *(Offering plate to* GOLD*)* Do you use butter or Vaseline?

GOLD: For what?

LE CROIX: For the goddamn tube.

GOLD: *(Deadpan)* Graphite like the locksmiths. Or perhaps in your case a shoehorn. Are you on medication?

LE CROIX: *(Eating)* Yes.

GOLD: May I see the prescription?

(MATI *brings in bag. Her eyes fixed upon* GOLD)

LE CROIX: Sometimes morphine, mostly heroin...for the pain.

GOLD: How long have you been taking heroin?

LE CROIX: Since my illness. NO tolerance for pain. Needles used to frighten me. Now they are my dearest friends.

GOLD: Who prescribed heroin?

LE CROIX: Who else? God.

GOLD: There are other painkillers.

LE CROIX: There are other doctors. Please eat.

(LE CROIX *coughs.* GOLD *takes out stethoscope.*)

LE CROIX: I like rock and roll. Like to dance and boogie. Fix me, Doctor. Take away my infirmity. Work your powerful magic. *(Removes shirt)* You're a good-looking man, Doctor. Do you work out?

GOLD: *(With stethoscope)* Breath normally.

LE CROIX: I grunt, cannot breath. My link with my great ancestors. I like the softness of your hands.

GOLD: Be still.

LE CROIX: Do you like black women?

GOLD: I'm married.

LE CROIX: Do you like black men?

GOLD: Your lungs are very weak.

LE CROIX: Is your sweet wife with you?

GOLD: When did you last take heroin?

LE CROIX: Yesterday morning upon rising.

GOLD: I want you off it immediately. If I'm to treat you, I can't have any nonsense. Understand?

LE CROIX: Withdrawal takes time. Hard to fight the devil's monkey. I'll cut down for you. You'll see.

GOLD: I want very clean blood samples. Beginning in five days.

LE CROIX: And golden urine samples? And pretty stools? I love Jewish doctors. So determined and professional. Do you like sports cars, my friend?

GOLD: *(Still examining)* Yes.

LE CROIX: And pornography? There's little pornography in Haiti unless you go online. Thanks to Jean-Bertrand Aristide. These fucking Catholic priests can drive you insane. The only smut on the newsstands is copies of Time magazine. I like smut. Gives the boys a rise. *(Prepares for blood test. Opens and closes fist)* For my detainees we provide lots of terrify smut on a flat screen T V. It's our way of humiliating them in the showers. The young men are raped by their first night—our special bridal suite—and their delicate rectums are ruptured by week's end. We hand out flowers and scented linen. Force them into our prestigious glee club, singing in French our best romantic folks songs.

GOLD: Your veins are punctured beyond recognition. You must be shooting up three times a day.

LE CROIX: Who counts? Do you find me attractive?

GOLD: No.

LE CROIX: Admit that you do.

GOLD: Are you homosexual, General?

LE CROIX: Because I wear eye shadow and mascara?

GOLD: So I see.

LE CROIX: It isn't manly, I know, but it brings out the best of me. Particularly with my riding boots on.

(GOLD *checks glands under his arms and chin*)

LE CROIX: I've a favorite leather coat I wear in cooler weather. Do you really think clothes make the man? How many nylons should an army officer wear? I bore you, Doctor. Pity. I can lecture about human rights and the haunting of Duvalier tyranny to this day. Would that entertain you? Shall I defend the rectitude of an electrode to a victim's testicle?

GOLD: You needn't bother.

LE CROIX: We seek converts, not confessions. Mandates, not elections.

GOLD: Why did you choose me, General?

LE CROIX: We have a file.

GOLD: Why me?

LE CROIX: Superstition. I wanted a Jew just as you are.

GOLD: I don't understand.

LE CROIX: I liked your photograph. You've a special talent for blending medical approaches. It's common knowledge. You take risks. Believe me, you do. Over all others in your field. Except the practitioners of voodoo. When I suffer detestable gas pains, I seek out the practitioner.

GOLD: How severe are the gas pains?

LE CROIX: Like earthquakes and tidal waves. I assure you, you may laugh at voodoo. Your medicine cannot comprehend it. Our island has such history. I cannot blame you for thinking modern. One must borrow from two worlds, Doctor. For gas and for lovesickness, I drink a concoction with entrails and monkey hair. Relief is guaranteed. I can be social again. A sick general must try every cure.

GOLD: You mustn't consult any more unlicensed doctors.

LE CROIX: What about Mati?

GOLD: Who is Mati?

LE CROIX: *(His hands caress* MATI*)* She attends to me.

GOLD: Does she give you medicine?

LE CROIX: Yes.

GOLD: I can't allow that. There'll be no other medical experts. Otherwise find another doctor.

LE CROIX: So strict, Doctor? Please be patient with little Jacques.

GOLD: You're an extreme egoist.

LE CROIX: And so are you, my friend. This is my birthright. I am Haiti. I like your presence. Don't bring your wife to our island. I am a jealous man. Don't ask me why. Tell her to stay with the children. Tell her there's miserable food in all our restaurants. You don' need undue distractions. You don't need your wife, Doctor.

GOLD: Get dressed.

LE CROIX: So quick?

GOLD: I'm expected back at the hospital.

LE CROIX: By helping our little Haitian children, you may wear the robe of the Messiah?

GOLD: I care about the children.

LE CROIX: How sweet. A new American program for our malnutrition.

GOLD: A damn good one, General.

LE CROIX: *Plus ça change, plus c'est la même chose.* Everything American, gives us much to cheer, Doctor.

GOLD: I'll continue the examination tomorrow. No more blindfolds. Is that clear, General?

LE CROIX: *(Whistling softly)* Look at my supple body. Linger and flirt.

GOLD: *(Trying to exit, MATI blocks him.)* You'll excuse me now.

LE CROIX: Look at my legs and elegant long hands. El Greco could paint my fingers. *(Primping)* Look at my Botticelli dimples. Look at my well-shaped buttocks. Can you tell that I ride horseback?

GOLD: No.

LE CROIX: Have you no imagination, man? *(Dances)* Look at this grace. Tell me that I'm exquisite.

GOLD: *(Ironic)* Would that please you?

LE CROIX: Must you ask?

Scene Three

(A cruise ship at sea off Port-au-Prince. On deck. A day later. Afternoon)

GOLD: I did get about a dozen soldiers the next day.

LATCH: Really?

GOLD: He kept his word. Hospital security has improved one hundred percent.

LATCH: I'd be surprised if this continues.

GOLD: He's in the habit of sending me flowers and champagne. It's rather embarrassing. He's offered a bullet-proof limousine too, but I really don't think that's necessary.

LATCH: Le Croix has taken a liking to you.

GOLD: Marvelous.

LATCH: Lovely fellow. Knows every opera by Wagner. Did he mention La Scala?

GOLD: No.

LATCH: Do you wonder why we are meeting like this?

GOLD: Yes.

LATCH: Safety.

GOLD: I see.

LATCH: The island's not safe, Doctor.

GOLD: Why isn't it safe?

LATCH: Don't you read the newspapers? The relief effort is a sham. Tremendous social unrest. Wyclef Jean's singing and stunts add up to a hill of beans. I don't mean to distract you from your critical study, but it's vital to get an intimate view of Le Croix.

GOLD: I didn't come here to work for the State Department.

LATCH: I realize, Doctor. Milk will save half of the impoverished world. Your milk. You have wonderful taste in leisure wear. I myself go in for Bill Blass. Muted pastels, pleated trousers. Silks and hand-washables for travel.

GOLD: Listen, McGuire...

LATCH: Call me Latch. My operative here. We're not in Washington.

GOLD: Latch, I can't afford to be away from the hospital for more than an hour.

LATCH: One of my men will drive you back when we dock.

GOLD: I don't like this runaround.

LATCH: We are asking you to check out Le Croix for a very essential reason. There is sufficient evidence to fear this man. He is an enemy of our country. We get this from our Intel. Because he's seeking medical assistance, you are our best cover for this investigation.

Just one or two more visits to his office, Doctor. You needn't do anything out of the ordinary. We trust you. You are our man in Port-au-Prince.

GOLD: This has nothing to do with my research.

LATCH: We are your sponsors. Since I went to bat for you at the N I H. you've had carte blanche. A small favor is all we ask in return. Just be our eyes and ears for a few more visits. I know you find this awkward. But it is, after all, for our country's well being. You did serve in the military...

GOLD: No.

LATCH: 4-F?

GOLD: I'm not military, Latch. Get with it.

LATCH: Every American should serve in the armed forces. I was a Marine. One hundred one-arm push-ups. To this day. I'm not a pussy, Doctor. God help the man who calls me a pussy. When do you meet with Le Croix again?

GOLD: Next week.

LATCH: Ask to see the detention center.

GOLD: Why?

LATCH: Just for your own curiosity. Go see the prison. And continue to treat him. We want him well.

Scene Four

(LE CROIX's *office. A week later.* MATI *is present in a corner of the room.* LE CROIX *enters with* GOLD.)

LE CROIX: We call it our Club Med facility. Do you like the décor?

GOLD: Don't you feel for these people at all?

LE CROIX: I do, actually. But we don't coddle terrorists and your country has mishandled terrorists too. Abu Ghraib photos, Doctor Gold? Corporal punishment is too gentle for these creatures. Far better to introduce them to the rigors of my exercise machines. Church officials do visit us. And by law. They're not shocked by the conditions. Secretly, I think they endorse such theories of correction. The Catholic church can mean business. Authority is either a thing of respect or it is nothing. *(Coughing)* I showed you the prison. I've no joy for euphemisms. My training is dedicated to Papa Doc. My politics ares something else. Why give prisoners shoes when a barefoot priest calls? Why separate homosexuals when your company is better than solitude. Why provide bedding and electricity when we don't run hotels? Are we in the business to please?

GOLD: What business are you in?

LE CROIX: To entertain the naughty boys.

GOLD: You didn't have to show me the facility.

LE CROIX: I thought you were curious. Forgive me, Doctor Gold. We have political adversaries. That is threatening. People are trying to kill me. No secret. My enemies are decadent. I maintain an ounce of integrity however. You look upset.

GOLD: Yes, I am.

LE CROIX: Something I said?

GOLD: Do you keep a file on me?

LE CROIX: Why do you ask?

GOLD: You do.

LE CROIX: Your file? Certainly, Doctor. *(Opens desk drawer)* This is your file. Shall I read from it? It is a detailed file. Doctor Jules Morris Gold...had a very upsetting childhood. Was molested in middle school. Has a fear of heights. Graduated Magna cum laude. Was married twice. Has a weakness for...shall I read on?

GOLD: No.

LE CROIX: I've a lot of material in this file. It shows that you too are important. To me. I can never find you at the children's hospital. I would like to have you on twenty-four hour call.

GOLD: I'm running between my lab and the hospital every day. Things are getting difficult at the hospital. We can't handle the crowds and the fighting. Your men are not doing enough.

LE CROIX: It looks like a violent year for all of us. There are natural hurricanes and man-made ones. You're very courageous to stay on the island.

GOLD: I've news of the tests.

LE CROIX: Yes?

GOLD: Your cancer isn't the chief problem.

LE CROIX: But I have cancer?

GOLD: Yes, a portion of the stomach wall can be removed surgically. It's an early stage. On the other hand, there are problems in your blood tests. The lymphatic development under your arms and neck is from a rare infection. I have never seen this condition before. It's not H I V, but something in that orbit.

LE CROIX: Can this be treated?

GOLD: I'm not the specialist you need.

LE CROIX: You cannot cure me?

GOLD: I can refer you to an American hospital. You'll have to fly to Miami. You can experiment with medication and perhaps radiation therapy. That's all I can suggest.

LE CROIX: I know your reputation. You can help me here. I cannot go to Florida. If you do not cure me, you are choosing to let me die.

GOLD: No, General.

LE CROIX: In your eyes I am a leper.

GOLD: Absolutely not.

LE CROIX: You think my life-style created this poor health?

GOLD: No one can answer that. But your condition will deteriorate within the year.

LE CROIX: I order you to import the medication and treat me here.

GOLD: I must return to my practice and to my family.

LE CROIX: After you cure me. You're supposed to be a miracle worker. Work one, Doctor. I want to live. I expect great changes in my Haiti. You must know I love my island. Other doctors told me about my condition, but you are not like other doctors. You have a passion quite different. I sense you have the cure. *(Pause)* Please, you will cure me.

Scene Five

(On board the cruise ship off Port-au-Prince. Some days later. Evening)

LATCH: Champagne?

GOLD: No, thank you.

LATCH: Did you vomit?

GOLD: Yes.

LATCH: I trust you're feeling better? Towards the bluffs, you can see the lights of a major installation. We're very alarmed by it. *(Pause)* How was your meeting with Le Croix?

GOLD: What do you expect me to say?

LATCH: The group behind Le Croix is no better than Duvalier's and less charming than Castro's. I see no reason to make things simple for these thugs. Goddamn voodoo communists. We take them quite seriously, Doctor. *(Silence)* I'm very sorry about your milk study. It must be a terribly blow to you.

GOLD: It is.

LATCH: How may infants did you lose?

GOLD: Seven.

LATCH: A singular tragedy.

GOLD: Yes.

LATCH: Pity. Such is the risk of medical experiments. One can't play God when there's filth and incompetence in these pisspot hospitals. With all these barefoot peasants sneaking into your ward. It's no reflection on your brilliance, Doctor. You wake up, look in the mirror, tell yourself the situation was less than ideal. You needn't worry, by friend, about this mishap.

GOLD: Last night I went to the homes of each family involved in the study. You cannot image the shame I felt. I couldn't say anything pleasant. I don't know what went wrong. These are all healthy babies.

LATCH: Yes.

GOLD: I shut down the entire wing of the hospital to spare the other infants. Then you people came in, before dawn, and reopened the ward.

LATCH: Of course.

GOLD: Bribing the hospital staff, giving me orders, and then I watch you pay these families to remain silent.

LATCH: To protect you.

GOLD: I don't need protection.

LATCH: But you do, from prosecution and from reprisals. You'll have full immunity and bodyguards too. No one will know about the milk study. We've cleared things with the local authorities and the media. Again, only to protect you. With a scandal like, you could lose your license. But we can stil be of assistance to each other.

GOLD: You don't own me, Latch.

LATCH: Trouble's brewing, Doctor. I need to ask for one more favor. We want Le Croix dead. We want you to kill him for us.

GOLD: You're out of your mind.

LATCH: Someone must kill him.. We've chosen you.

GOLD: You asked me to save his life.

LATCH: I've gotten word from Washington, Doctor. High up. Quip pro quo.

GOLD: My patriotism stops short of murder.

LATCH: He's a reach charmer, isn't he? Reads Nazi literature at his bedside. Tortures Jews, intellectuals, homosexuals, Starbucks representatives, dissident teenagers. Castrates any creature who crosses him. A real charmer. And queer as a three dollar bill. Don't you feel moral anger? For an officer of a developing nation, Le Croix has ha a highly developed rectum. We wouldn't be surprised to find a cruise missile somewhere inside him.

GOLD: I don't like blackmail.

LATCH: I understand how you feel. You were very kind to treat him in the first place. But many people will die if Le Croix comes to power. We have no one else to turn to. We are very sorry to kill him, Doctor *(Pouring champagne)* If you had served in the military, you'd have no qualms about such actions. Sometimes a man must take action. Certainly a patriot. Pretend you're James Bond, in black tie and on location, with a specially prepared hypodermic. Even your cantankerous victim will thank you. And afterwards we will continue to protect you. For the rest of your life. How rough and beautify the sea looks tonight. How I love the sea.

GOLD: Nothing feels safe.

LATCH: You don't trust me?

GOLD: No.

LATCH: Because you're in a state of shock, Doctor. It's only natural to fee confused a day after tragedy. Unfortunately, we've no one else to turn to. He accepts you into his compound without bodyguard. Acceptance is the hardest part. Let down your guard with him. You're in no danger. On my mother's grave. He tends to be enthusiastic at this phase of a crush.

GOLD: What's that supposed to mean?

LATCH: Buddy-buddy. Physical camaraderie.

GOLD: Go fuck yourself.

LATCH: It's so simple, Doctor. Just give him the needle. He loves needles.

GOLD: Le Croix's illness is terminal. Let him die in his own way.

LATCH: We can't wait. Four weeks. I get my orders from a very high authority.

GOLD: For you, life is cheap, Latch.

LATCH: You buy life with cash. Love with nylons. Friends with favors. God with a donation.

GOLD: And if I just return to New York?

LATCH: Without completing the assignment? Well, I'll lose my Christmas bonus, and you'll wish you were dead.

Scene Six

(The balcony of GOLD's villa in Haiti. Some weeks later. January. Morning. JO ANNE is alone viewing the city. GOLD joins her. They are in house robes.)

JO ANNE: I heard gunshots earlier.

GOLD: It's normal throughout the day. Looters...

JO ANNE: Hangover?

GOLD: Yes.

JO ANNE: You passed out last night.

GOLD: Did I?

JO ANNE: You've lost weight. Look haggard actually.

GOLD: I'm sorry if I do. I'm missing meals.

JO ANNE: Judging by the empties in the hall, it seems you're doing some serious drinking in your fancy little shanty.

GOLD: It helps pass the time.

JO ANNE: This is not like you.

GOLD: Would you like breakfast? Coffee? *(Silence)* I'm surprised to see you here.

JO ANNE: I could have come two weeks ago. You blocked me. Why the hell are you still here?

GOLD: Orders from the State Department.

JO ANNE: What are you doing for them? You're milk study's over.

GOLD: I'm not permitted to say.

JO ANNE: Not even to your wife? *(Silence)* They've talked to me, Jules. Before I left New York. I don't like them. Are they controlling you?

GOLD: No.

JO ANNE: Someone's controlling you.

GOLD: Mephistopheles.

JO ANNE: *(Staring at the city view)* It's a filthy rancid island. At least from my eyes. Such poverty and depravity. Human hell. I pity these people. Your new home, Jules? I was attached yesterday at the airport. For no reason. While crossing the street, a woman grabbed my hat and purse. She slapped me. I was going to tell you this last night but you weren't listening to me.

(Sirens heard.)

JO ANNE: Seeing you like this is unnerving, Jules. Come home with me. I'll help you pack.

GOLD: I can't go, Jo Anne.

JO ANNE: What is your commitment here? Answer me? I want an answer.

GOLD: The whole city is seething. The island is in final decay. One can sense the hidden choreographic hand of evil at work. One ignited match and we'll have human fireworks.

JO ANNE: Come home with me, darling. This is killing you.

GOLD: Another week and I'm free.

JO ANNE: I've been to the hospital. I know about the infants.

GOLD: Go home, Jo Anne.

JO ANNE: You must be in a lot of pain. Come home. Our children want you home.

GOLD: I killed those babies. My own formula. My life's work. Finished. They autopsy of career. Images of infants in canvas body bags. Well, I think my magic formula was really meant for me.

JO ANNE: The study was experimental and you had substandard institutional support.

GOLD: I was responsible for everything. I set the standards.

JO ANNE: You're not God.

GOLD: I can't bear myself, Jo Anne. Can't you understand that?

JO ANNE: I do, darling. Let's pack and fly today.

GOLD: I can't.

JO ANNE: Is this Le Croix so important? Why must you see him? I've been briefed.

GOLD: Jo Anne, this is all too dangerous.

JO ANNE: Why must you treat him?

GOLD: Because he's dying and I am his physician.

JO ANNE: With certain drugs?

GOLD: Yes.

JO ANNE: Killer drugs?

GOLD: What the good doctor ordered. *Primum non nocere.* First do no harm. The physician's credo. You've seen me at my worst. I'm fascinated by him, yet I know he is despicable

JO ANNE: You're risking your life.

GOLD: I don't give a damn. I'll lose my license to practice. I'll be the medical idiot in all the tabloids. I can pick up the syringe.

JO ANNE: Our government cannot do this to you.

GOLD: Furst would call it zugzwang. Doomed to move, doomed to stay. Paralyzed like a tortoise supine. What ridiculous indignity. I've dreams each night of someone unscrewing my head like a bottle top. Sucking my guts out. Literally being turned inside out. Zugzwang. Checkmate. Unless I cheat. Isn't it better to prove patriotic?

JO ANNE: Jules, come to your senses. Wake up. Leave with me.

GOLD: With you?

JO ANNE: With me. Yes, Damnit. I love you.

(More gunfire)

GOLD: I love you.

JO ANNE: They've scarred you. I don't know what else to say. You took an oath...physician, husband, father. Honor the oath.

GOLD: I promise to leave by the end of the week. Then the nightmare will end. I give you my promise.

JO ANNE: I may not be home for you when you decide to return.

GOLD: You'll be there waiting for me. We have roles to play. I want your support.

JO ANNE: Get out of this godforsaken place, Jules. I'm flying back tonight. There's a reservation for two. I love you, darling. I love you with all my life. That is my support.

Scene Seven

(Aboard ship. Some days later. Evening)

LATCH: You're drinking more these days.

GOLD: Yes.

LATCH: Your wife is very attractive. It was a pleasure to meet her. I regret she heard more than she should. We had to debrief her again at the airport. You must miss her terribly. I wish I were married, Doctor. A bachelor's life can be misery. *(Silence)* Because of the riots, the Haitian authorities have asked for emergency assistance and American troops. It's time to take out the General.

GOLD: Why take sides? Le Croix is not the only thug in Haiti.

LATCH: You're wrong, Doctor. We must stabilize Haiti.

GOLD: You mean sodomize Haiti.

LATCH: To pick the players, one should really study the scorecard.

GOLD: You're about as manly as a cardboard cutout.

LATCH: I really wish we had more time to chat, Doctor but I've been pushed to the wire. By now, you should find ample reason to execute Le Croix. You know him. You've power over him. He's slated to die from poor health, so this is not a sin. *(Hands over paper)* We want him dead tomorrow. Here's your shopping list. Make it look like a drug overdose. There will be an autopsy. Tomorrow, Doctor Gold. It will be very hard to leave the island without our help.

GOLD: You're very good at details, Latch.

LATCH: Thank you. I live for details. Just as a physician lives for a reputation.

GOLD: To hell with all that.

LATCH: Be sober tomorrow. It'd be careless to look unprofessional and tip him off. Our men will run you directly to the airport after Le Croix. Please follow their instructions. After today, you and I will not meet anymore. *(Pause)* You are an outstanding American, my friend. You singlehandedly saved the Haitian world.

GOLD: Tell me something...

LATCH: What?

GOLD: Which of your men tainted my infant testing?

Scene Eight

(LE CROIX's office. The next day. MATI, alone, dances and drops powder in the form of a protective circle. She exits. GOLD and LE CROIX enter. During the following dialogue, MATI, reenters stealthily.)

GOLD: Medication.

LE CROIX: For me?

GOLD: Yes.

LE CROIX: You've changed your mind?

GOLD: Yes.

LE CROIX: Why?

GOLD: I've an experimental drug. You're worth the effort. This may turn the tide.

LE CROIX: How experimental?

GOLD: It has been successful with various tropical infections and as long as your H I V is inhibited—I believe we can fend off your other blood problem. The serum may even build up your immune system. I've only tried it on laboratory animals. This is what it is, General. As with any new drug there is a large risk.

I think it's worth the risk, but you must make that decision.

LE CROIX: Any side effects?

GOLD: Loss of hair, appetite, sleeplessness, temporary impotency. Maybe a burning session when you urinate. Again, all worth the effort.

LE CROIX: How many injections?

GOLD: Once a week. For several months. Your army surgeon can repeat this injection after I'm gone.

LE CROIX: You are homesick.

GOLD: Yes.

LE CROIX: You could live with me in the presidential palace. I will be Haiti's next President. You can watch life from my review stand. Be my confidant.

GOLD: That's exceedingly kind of you, General.

LE CROIX: Live with me, Doctor.

GOLD: You hate Jews, yet you continue to favor me.

LE CROIX: I deplore venereal disease but I'm drawn to sex.

GOLD: With all due respect, General, you're appalling.

LE CROIX: I have a twelve-inch cock.

GOLD: Congratulations.

LE CROIX: Flatter me, Doctor.

GOLD: I would prefer to kill you.

LE CROIX: Kill me in bed, Doctor. Between the satin sheets. My humor now offends you?

GOLD: Not at all.

LE CROIX: (Watching GOLD prepare the injection) When are you leaving, Doctor?

GOLD: In a few days.

LE CROIX: This is very sad news. I'm sincere. I care for you. I will miss you with all my heart.

GOLD: I doubt you will.

LE CROIX: I will miss you.

GOLD: And I'll miss you too. The long country rides in your jeep and the painted skulls along your corridor. The medication may make your heart palpitate. It could even kill you.

LE CROIX: Nothing in a syringe can kill me.

GOLD: Roll up your sleeve.

LE CROIX: If all goes well, how long will I live?

GOLD: Sixteen months? Six years? Until old age sets in?

LE CROIX: You make me feel like a prisoner to my emotions. You tested me, inspected me. A guinea pig in love with a man of mystery. A master in white. You must feel what I feel. You cannot deny a certain passion, Doctor. I look out my window and see U S wartime ships.

GOLD: There are no American ships.

LE CROIX: Not today. But there will come a time.

GOLD: Roll up your sleeve, General.

LE CROIX: I sense power oozing out of my loins. Whores bite me when my vitality fails. I could set all my shitty prisoners free. Clemency comes once in a lifetime. I once loved my Cuban barber. Like you, he told me to get rid of my drugs. Like you, he told me to empty the jails. He used to powder my neck, dress me, escort me, hold me in his strong Cuban arms. Knew my vulnerability. My silly fantasies. Bathed me with his sentimental tears. Would sterilize my syringe in barber's water. Would kiss me deeply with tender words of love. How I mourn his death.

GOLD: Roll up your sleeve. Please.

LE CROIX: Do you think I'm afraid of your treatment? I see my coffin and pale wilting flowers. In hell, the Haitian hatcheck girl tips the patron. Why am I so fearful, Doctor? Why do you make me so tender? Can't you see that now? Are you blinded by some narcotic too? In your mind I'm a vicious torturer of the innocent. No one is innocent. Not even you.

GOLD: *(Completes the injection, wipes skin clean)* My job is done, General. Relax. Stay calm.

LE CROIX: Exorcise me, Doctor. Heal me from my sins. What's the Jewish word for cleansing the soul? *(Grabs GOLD's arm suddenly)* Tell me the Hebrew words!

GOLD: Let go of me.

LE CROIX: You are a lapsed Jew. You pray to a god who speedballs. A narcissistic god deadened by morphine and false praise. Modern man like you, stooped posture, with a religious rag on your head. You pretend to fast in October, eating bacon in the dark. Lie in my bed, man. I'll show you Jesus Christ.

GOLD: I can't hear anymore of this.

LE CROIX: I know.

GOLD: In all my years in medicine I've never seen a man such as you.

LE CROIX: Is it my politics or my gender or the color of human stain? Let me rest my head up on your shoulder. I'm feeling weak.

GOLD: I hope you respond to the drug. It should comfort you.

LE CROIX: Yes, I do feel it, man.

GOLD: Good. Put your mind on pleasant things. Imagine a world as gentle as a cloud.

LE CROIX: You have an exceptional bedside manner, Doctor. That has to be love. *(Silence. Just as he seems to fall off into unconscious, he stirs)* I...I have a secret to tell. I know what's inside the syringe..

GOLD: What do you know?

LE CROIX: I know too much. The failure of your medical study. The infant deaths. I know your operatives. I know your wife. I know how to dance. Come dance with me. You've captured my intimacy. Fought my addiction with this visit today. Obedient boy. Found me with my trousers down. My bullock scrotum to the wind. When your hands grazed my bare chest, I could not resist. How foolish I felt. Dear God, another handsome Jewish doctor. You circumcised my heart. You owe me a kindness.

GOLD: Do I?

LE CROIX: A whisper for my wounds. Come closer, Doctor.

GOLD: I must go.

LE CROIX: I will follow you. I will follow you everywhere. *(Faint, slouches in chair)*

GOLD: You need your rest. No more talking.

LE CROIX: *(Slurred)* Sing me a lullaby. Let me pass gently.

GOLD: Are you in pain?

LE CROIX: Yes.

GOLD: I feel pain too.

LE CROIX: God's chosen. The gross Haitian and the woven Jew. Come embrace me, Doctor. Before death. I might as well be a Jew, wrapped in white prayer. Le mariee est trop belle. The bride is too beautiful. My head is full of camphor. Put on your fanciest wedding jacket, dearest, and claim this corpse.

GOLD: *(Tenderly)* Sleep eternal, General.

LE CROIX: *(Eyes shut)* Yes, I feel it working finally.
The hot curdling liquids looking for the special seed.
Microbes fleeing. Scum churning clean. Where is my
virgin bride? And the simple Jewish canopy? *(In softest
voice)* Marry me, sweet doctor, marry me. *(Passes out)*

Scene Nine

*(GOLD's home. End of January. Many things in disarray.
GOLD in involved in three separate meta-realistic dialogues
at rapid clip)*

FURST: I missed you, Julies. You're so gaunt and pale.
Where is your Caribbean tan?

GOLD: In my valise.

FURST: Is this a depression, Jules?

GOLD: You don't email or phone.

FURST: I can't email anymore. You said you'd be back
by December. How was your study?

GOLD: *(Unfocused)* Two weeks here, and still can't find
the glasses she packed. Makes no sense. Silverware.
China. All packed up. How's Jo Anne?

FURST: Must you ask?

     *   *   *

JO ANNE: Jules, you made everyone sound the Big
Brass Alarm. When is this binge over?

GOLD: You know I can't cook.

JO ANNE: After Ludwig's call, I became worried.

GOLD: Worry for me?

JO ANNE: Don't stare, Jules. It's hard enough to be here
at all. Very tidy.

GOLD: The cleaning girl comes Thursdays. Do the children miss me?

JO ANNE: Yes.

GOLD: Where are you staying?

JO ANNE: I must keep my distance, Jules. You're dangerous.

GOLD: Who's coaching you? Ludwig or your analyst?

JO ANNE: No one's coaching me.

   *   *   *

SHIRLEY: How should I understand things?

JO ANNE: Many years ago I courted fantasies. It was my background. The whiteness of medicine, Shirley. The cleanliness of ministry.

SHIRLEY: Jules, you're very mixed up.

GOLD: Don't take sides.

SHIRLEY: I don't.

GOLD: You do. You've opinions. My wife shuns me as though I were a leper. I came back to inhabit a custom-made tomb.

SHIRLEY: I've talked to her, Jules. Your marriage is slipping away. On occasion you do listen to me.

GOLD: Don't bait me, Shirley.

   *   *   *

GOLD: I can't find my dress shirts, or my black bag. I'm afraid to drive the car past the mailbox. When you came to Haiti, I was lacking something. The human mind is exceptionally elastic. I forgive you, Jo Anne, for your excesses, for your middle-class habits, for your emotionalism. You still mean the world to me. For I too am hopelessly middle-class and middlebrow.

SHIRLEY: I want the house, Jules. As soon as you get yourself together, find another address.

GOLD: Am I beyond forgiveness?

JO ANNE: You're like a child flouting curfew. You leave a room, and all of us disappear. You make me so empty inside. You're back home, but not really. Someone is living inside you

GOLD: I love you, darling.

JO ANNE: You make me feel so empty. I pray for you.

*   *   *

GOLD: I had brighter expectations.

FURST: How clean were the labs?

GOLD: Satisfactory after the first week.

FURST: Listeriosis?

GOLD: The upshot is their immune system failed.

FURST: Did you file your report?

GOLD: Jo Anne won't return my calls.

FURST: What does the N I H say?

GOLD: She left in the middle of the night. Little notes around the house. All her things gone. Her clothes, her shoes, the exercycle.

FURST: After so many months, what the hell did you expect?

*   *   *

SHIRLEY: Something shocked Jo Anne in Haiti. Her instincts play havoc on her. I've had disturbing dreams about your deals.

GOLD: What do you know?

SHIRLEY: When I feed the morning birds, they tell me secrets. If I don't feed the birds, they wait dangerously

along power lines. Make a full admission. It is too plain
to see.

GOLD: There's nothing to admit.

SHIRLEY: There are telltale signs, Jules, of mortal crimes.

GOLD: God is a criminal, Shirley. We are all bystanders.

*   *   *

JO ANNE: I've hired a lawyer.

GOLD: Must we deal with lawyers?

JO ANNE: Mediation is the other route.

GOLD: I came back to a ghost house.

JO ANNE: I have to protect myself.

GOLD: Let's rebuild our marriage.

JO ANNE: You tie to yourself, you tie to me.

GOLD: Say yes, goddamn it. Give me a second chance.

JO ANNE: Speak to my lawyer, Jules.

GOLD: My intentions were noble.

JO ANNE: I am not Mother Teresa.

FURST, JO ANNE, & SHIRLEY: Watching you slip into
such an endless hole, Jules...

JO ANNE: ...wondering how did this every happen to
us?

*   *   *

FURST: Call the hospital board, if you doubt me. You
need protection, Jules. Schler covets your practice
and your position. You've come back with shattered
humility. Tell what you want tour medical community.
I won't dispute you. Your place is by my side. Until I
die. My pledge to you.

*   *   *

SHIRLEY: Look at me, Jules. My marvelous life with Ludwig made me receive things hidden to others. How beguiling to wait for sparrows before the first cup of black coffee. Can I pretend I didn't see your black leather bag spilling entrails and organs across Port-au-Prince?

GOLD: Help me.

SHIRLEY: I'm not political but what unruly monsters there are in politics. Extend your hand. Trust me. As God is my witness, you're running out of time.

*   *   *

GOLD: Make love to me.

JO ANNE: All that is forbidden. Look away. Look away. You had energy for living. How I misse that, Jules. You've no idea what things I do miss.

GOLD: I'll get professional help.

JO ANNE: I wish you well.

GOLD: I'll quit my practice. Give me some encouragement.

JO ANNE: To what purpose?

GOLD: To save a life.

*   *   *

SHIRLEY: Can you believe in Him now?

GOLD: I believe in God's mellifluous torture. We are sport amusement. Creatures of derision and dung appetite. The question is if God feels embarrassment at his sublime creation?

SHIRLEY: Let God inside.

GOLD: Children wait for God.

SHIRLEY: There's grace to make a change.

GOLD: Absolution? I know my heart, Shirley. I know what's inside.

SHIRLEY: Heal thyself. I pray for you, Jules, how I pray for things to be made right.

    *   *   *

(In this final dialogue, now breaking from the previous text, has naturalistic, unrushed pacing)

JO ANNE: I should go now.

GOLD: Don't go, I beg you.

(GOLD kisses JO ANNE. She is motionless.)

GOLD: You've changed your perfume.

JO ANNE: Yes.

GOLD: I like it. You look smashing.

JO ANNE: Take care, Jules.

GOLD: Jo Anne?

JO ANNE: *(Exiting)* Yes?

GOLD: *(Steps towards her)* I feel very optimistic.

JO ANNE: *(Sadly)* Yes, Jules. The sky's dropping rose petals.

Scene Ten

(GOLD's home. The next day. LE CROIX lounges on the couch, his luggag and paraphernalia everywhere. The space is as much Haitian as American. LE CROIX is in garish civilian clothes. GOLD, entering from his bedroom, halts.)

LE CROIX: The door was open, so I let myself in.

GOLD: Get out.

LE CROIX: Is this hospitality? I traveled thousands of miles to see you. Are you surprised to see little

Jacques? I issed my daily checkups. Didn't you? How long have you been in my thoughts. Shall I undress?

GOLD: Get out of my house.

LE CROIX: It's snowing outside. Look out the window, man. I've never seen such lovely white flakes. Look out, you'll see Mati in the black limousine. We drove up for you.

GOLD: How dare you...

LE CROIX: Be gracious, Doctor.

GOLD: Why are you here?

LE CROIX: Why am I alive?

GOLD: The serum is working.

LE CROIX: Yes, is it not a happy event?

GOLD: My work is completed and we can part company.

LE CROIX: Au contraire.

GOLD: You think I meant you harm.

LE CROIX: No, no, no. You are a sweet physician. Come, give a warm embrace to beau beau. You saved my life.

GOLD: It's through the grace of Heaven.

LE CROIX: Yes, I keep telling myself that. But you look so wan and tired. How about a Creole meal? Have you had dinner? Good. I'll call Mati inside. She loves to cook.

GOLD: The fridge is empty.

LE CROIX: We've groceries in the car.

(MATI *enters with groceries. She is in western dress.*)

Ah, Mati...come in. You remember Doctor Gold. He made house calls. Why not prepare a Creole meal for us. Does the doctor like snails? What wonders she does with snails. No butter sauce. No garlic. No cholesterol. Other juices. Are you kosher, Doctor?

GOLD: No.

LE CROIX: Splendid. She knows only one way of cooking. Washing the food in deep basins, fighting flies, Creole in the air. Chattering to a ragman who will do your bidding. His wares are for sale. A festival in Haiti. Native drums pounding in the distance. Rhythms snake through the parched red soil. Colored banners and masks. Roosters push at small children in the market square. *Au revoir,* Ibo. Yanvalu, our Vodun evocation dance. *(Approaches* GOLD*)* Besides cooking up a storm, Mati likes to raise the dead. A skill which runs in her family. Shall we dance Yanvalu, a very slow poetic dance?

GOLD: No.

LE CROIX: May I teach you?

GOLD: I'm very clumsy on two feet.

LE CROIX: Can that be? You seem so light on your feet and so fleeting. I like your house. I do. So well appointed. A standard of living for a Jewish Prince. Your wife's fine taste? The austerity of modern art? Have you a wine cellar? We've many rare vintages in the car. A bottle to celebrate?

GOLD: Why bother?

LE CROIX: No bother, man.

GOLD: Why come here?

LE CROIX: You gave me no choice.

GOLD: Is that a threat?

LE CROIX: No, a joke. Do you get the joke?

GOLD: What's the joke?

LE CROIX: I am not dead. That's the joke.

GOLD: You've enough chemicals to knock out an army.

LE CROIX: Yes, I sometimes feel like a large test tube from Du Pont. Did you make your government happy? Is it good to be a soldier without uniform?

(MATI, *who has exited to the kitchen, reenters with tray and syringe.)*

Good, Mati. Let's make it a short one. I'm feeling a migraine coming on. *(Rolls up sleeve, slaps vein, ties cord around arm)* Excuse me, Doctor.

(MATI *injects* LE CROIX. *He stretches out, high on the climb.* MATI *returns to kitchen.)*

It's a thing of beauty to leek like a dead man with eagle wings, soaring over dark forbidden ravines. I offer you some. Come, my brother. Gros mosso. I feel no pain. Misery can be cured in the best of style Haut gout. High taste. A very slight decay. I offer you some.

GOLD: No.

LE CROIX: It gives me faith in the unknown. Love for borrowed time. So come now. Roll up your sleeve.

GOLD: I don't take needles.

LE CROIX: Just share one with me. Just for company's sake.

GOLD: I am not company.

LE CROIX: Then what are you?

GOLD: I was your doctor.

LE CROIX: You were my assassin. Truly. My doctor assassin. My angel of mercy. Your government doctored your milk. And you doctored my medication. Roll up your sleeve, mon ami.

GOLD: Heroin makes you psychotic.

LE CROIX: You put cameras in my rectum, drop leaflets in my soup. Why?

GOLD: I see the world as you do.

LE CROIX: You're so seductive, Doctor. They've tried other doctors, but you were the first to get close. Blame yourself, or blame your masters. It's all the same to me. I accept exile. Mati and I like to masquerade. Wonderful to read your own obituary. Soon we will dine. I am famished. I don't plan to leave your home. I've enough morphine for eternity. (*Feeling faint*) Call Mati.

GOLD: Are you all right?

LE CROIX: Tell her to plug me once again. Opium.

GOLD: You'll overdose.

LE CROIX: Nonsense. Nothing in a syringe can kill me. Mati knows Vodun. I trust her to find me wherever I fall. Her bronze arms are sinewy, but reach out as far as the eye can see. She has selected a sublime hole in the earth. A most beautiful location. We will drive there this week. You won't be disappointed.

(MATI *enters with a tray of food, sets it on table in dining room.* LE CROIX *ignores her*)

LE CROIX: You look terrible, Doctor. Haven't you been eating? Are you fasting? I shall nurture you back to health. Give you strength and resolve. Wait and see. Where are you children? And your wife? Would they not want to come to dinner?

GOLD: They're gone.

LE CROIX: I'm so sorry to hear this.

GOLD: I know my deeds.

LE CROIX: Then be glad to see me. Tell me you are glad.

GOLD: I just want solitude.

LE CROIX: Only the dead ask for solitude. I'm happy to see you. To see a humor buried between us. (*Watching*

MATI *set the table)* Help me, Doctor, to my feet. We may dine. Doctor?

*(*GOLD *approaches, helps* LE CROIX.)*

LE CROIX: Tell me a dirty story, man. Make a racial joke. Here we can be foolish with one another. I could play doctor, and you play general.

*(*LE CROIX *crosses with* GOLD *to table, about to sit.)*

LE CROIX: Sit, sit. Let's partake in a special feast. *(Throws napkin at* GOLD*)* That's all, Mati. Thank you.

*(*MATI *steps away from the table but lingers nearby.)*

LE CROIX: Pick up a fork, Doctor. You may serve.

GOLD: You must be indestructible, General.

LE CROIX: I am an army man.

GOLD: You defy logic.

LE CROIX: It would be a good thing. Fate was generous.

GOLD: All along you had expected me.

LE CROIX: Yes.

GOLD: I need a drink. *(About to rise)*

LE CROIX: Mati.

*(*MATI *brings over a bottle of Scotch.)*

LE CROIX: She is here to serve you.

*(*MATI *pours.* GOLD *drinks.)*

LE CROIX: I am here to entertain you.

GOLD: I don't want a dinner date.

LE CROIX: Eat Doctor Gold. Don't insult Mati.

*(*GOLD *eats)*

LE CROIX: The political embarrassments made the complexion of my skin change for the worse. Sometimes I imagine a cold draft on my shoulder

and see the hand of a skeleton. Driving north along
the Interstate, I ate three hundred pecan pies. We
pick up the car in Key West. Drove to Orland, a day
in Disneyworld, then Daytona, Virginia Beach, and
finally Washington DC... Mati did all the driving.
Skipped Atlantic City, but we did tour Manhattan. We
climbed the Empire State Building. What a magnificent
view. What a lovely country. How fortunate to be an
American with luxury autos, unctuous riches, and the
sense of permanent royalty. To see your home, I see
your entire life. Your wife left many notes for you.
How to use the washer-dryer. Luck can change for
winners. Relinquishing my command was an unhappy
task. I gave up the remains of my world. And by doing
so, the C I A can crow. The C I A can buy you like
merchandise.

GOLD: I am not merchandise. Why are you staring?

LE CROIX: How is your plate?

GOLD: All right.

LE CROIX: You barely eat.

GOLD: Forgive me.

LE CROIX: Did you ask your Ambassador to Haiti about
the shadow doctors that ruined your life?

(The telephone rings. GOLD stands, dizzy.)

GOLD: Excuse me.

LE CROIX: Are you all right?

GOLD: I don't know. *(Hands reach chair for support)*

LE CROIX: Sit, Doctor. You're peaked. *(Hands across the
table)* Drink some water.

GOLD: *(Sinking into seat)* I was about to black out.

(Telephone stops ringing.)

LE CROIX: You must lack sleep.

GOLD: Something is pricking through my stomach.

LE CROIX: You are unfamiliar with snails?

GOLD: Is this food clean?

LE CROIX: Clean?

GOLD: *(Eyes closing)* Is it clean?

LE CROIX: Yes, the food is clean. But we are not.

GOLD: *(Unable to see)* Why do this to me?

LE CROIX: I crave your company. I want your fidelity. I want you in my bosom for a thousand years.

GOLD: I tried to spare your life.

LE CROIX: Yes, you spared me an extra day. I feel like the woeful Oriental forever indebted to his savior from the West. You brought me a firm belief. For that I wish to repay you.

GOLD: *(In great pain)* You son-of-a-bitch!

LE CROIX: I'm right behind you, Doctor. Sleep soundly. Same fate, same pot of food. A grand finale. *(Reaches across table, hand over GOLD's)* No more instructions. Be mine.

(LE CROIX closes his eyes. We hear faraway drums and snow falls on the two men. Lights fade to blackout.)

END OF PLAY

www.ingramcontent.com/pod-product-compliance
Lightning Source LLC
Chambersburg PA
CBHW070029110426
42741CB00034B/2693